BLACK/WHITE

WE ARE NOT PANIC (PANDEMIC) FREE

10/7/20

To Michael,
In Friendship.

Elvis Alves BLM

Elvis Alves

ISBN 978-0-9884324-0-6

Book Design by Tishon Woolcock

WE ARE NOT PANIC (PANDEMIC) FREE

BLACK

WHITE

FAMILIARITY:

Buy what you usually get
from the store of life.

DISPLACEMENT:

Pivoting toward destruction.
Spot of unbecoming, where
self searches for location.

STATE SANCTIONED VIOLENCE:

- Police Brutality/Militarization of Police Force
- Prison Industrial Complex
- Defunding of Public Education
- No/Low Corporate Tax
- The Working Poor

NEVER FORGET:

**Amazon says books are
not essential during
the pandemic.**

GOD:

**The power within you,
and beyond the bullshit.**

PRAYER:

What we say to the self
when we talk to God.

(CHURCHES OF)
LALIBELA:

Reminder to respect the
earth even if you do not
worship it. Land of return
in Rastafarianism.

ARGUMENT FOR
SAFE REOPENING
OF SCHOOLS:

Closed Schools
=
Closed Minds

RECENT FAVORITE MOVIE:

**The Last Black Man in
San Francisco (2019).**

GENTRIFICATION:

Newcomers take
space from oldtimers
by any means necessary.

TOWER OF
BABEL:

Build words on tongue
that reach God.

TRUMP:

Dump him like a bad partner. Election 2020.

POWER:

The ability to
influence for
good or bad.

MARRIAGE:

History of compromises.
Bond of love.

SKYLARKING:

Bodies at rest or play in public. Not advisable now.

LITANY:

**Of tears too
much to bear.**

SUSAN RICE:

National Security Advisor under Obama. Left 69-page pandemic playbook ignored by Trump Administration.

**(UNSOLICITED)
ADVICE:**

There should be
no tolerance for
ignorance.

RAP:

Music of the
unheard until
commodified.

QUESTION FOR AMERICA:

**What would you do
if the pandemic is
here to stay like
racism?**

THE BRONX:

Has the most
COVID-19 cases
per capita. Poorest
borough in NYC.

REMITTANCES:

Money sent to one's country of origin (to help those left behind). Trump proposed disruption of this system in fight against illegal immigration.

REMDESIVIR:

Drug that shows
promise in fight
against COVID-19.
Dr. Fauci says it reminds
him of early fight
against HIV/AIDS.

PIER 39
(SUNSET PARK,
BROOKLYN):

There are makeshift
morgues at Pier 39 in
Brooklyn. Trump announces
plans to disband COVID-19
task force. He wants everyone
back at work.

AGONY:

Annoyance to the
umpteenth degree.
Beyond restlessness.
Existential angst +
more.

TROUBLED MAN:

**Trump seems to reverse
call to disband COVID-19
task force. Says he's
surprised by its popularity.**

**AIN'T THAT
THE TRUTH.
AFFIRMATION:**

**Black lives
matter in a
country that says
the opposite.**

**ON CUSP OF
REOPENING
STATE (NY):**

Gov. Cuomo says
that people who
have been practicing
social distancing and
staying at home had
the highest hospitalization
rate this week.

**BREAKING
NEWS:**

White House staffers test positive for COVID-19.

IN MEMORIAM:

I keep thinking I'd
see the young man
that died in my
building.

Existential angst will remain with us after the COVID-19 pandemic is over. It is part of the human condition. Perhaps the pandemic can help us see the structures in our society that contribute to panic, a phenomenon that is lessened if the structures are destroyed.

Elvis Alves is the author of Bitter Melon, Ota Benga, and I Am No Battlefield But A Forest Of Trees Growing. He lives in New York City with his family.

Made in the USA
Columbia, SC
25 September 2020